Skydive

By Jarrin Wooten

DEDICATION

To Dashonda, Annie, Alisha, Laportia, Justin, Trevion, Demetrius, Ci'Ana, and Cameron. I am nothing without any of you.

ACKNOWLEDGMENTS

To every muse that came in the form of family, friends, and
lovers of past and present, and future. Thank you for
allowing me to tell my story through our shared experiences.
I'm forever grateful

Contents

The Reason

I write to heal,
heal not only myself but others too
because after all the repairs,
I'm still broken.
I'm broken from feeling inferior
when all I needed was confidence,
broken from feeling rejected
when all I wanted was acceptance
Life a lot of times
was never a fairytale
And I'm still looking for promises
that were supposed to come with the change
I threw in wishing wells.
But until then,
Hopefully my words will continue to heal
not only myself but others too
and maybe the things I've gone through
will help with how you go through them too

I Was That Kid

I remember I was that kid
playing in the park.
Sand in my shoes and sweat from the sun
on my face from giving life my best chase
and time was an afterthought.
I thought I could do this forever.

I remember I was that kid
outside with my friends
that had to beat the sunlight in
It never crossed my mind that one day
when we played outside
it would be for the last time
I thought we'd be out here forever

I remember I was that kid,
fighting with my siblings all day
but if I knew that growing up
meant going our own separate ways
I'd be more mindful of how we played.
I thought we'd grow up together forever

I remember I was that kid
without a single care in the world
and life yet to live at my fingertips,
if what I know now was what was known then
I would have slowed down
And cherished growing up a little more
I thought I'd be that kid forever

When I'm Gone

I want trying to forget me
To be as difficult
as trying to remember a dream.

You can't see me anymore,
but you can never deny that I happened

Walls

I built this wall brick by brick

hoping that one day I'd feel safe.

See this wall is now my protection,

and I built it to stay away from identical mistakes.

The same mistakes that plagued my past when this wall didn't exist,

but the price of my purity turned out to be defenselessness.

I had nothing to block pain applied by people playing impostor parts in my life,

and now this wall reserves my heart's inhibitions for anybody that makes pursuing them a mission.

This wall is my refuge, yet my chaos.

My peace, yet my insanity.

My gift, and my curse.

Because as long as I keep everything out,

I can't let anything in.

Strong Friend

It's funny how
we never ask the therapist
if they need therapy.

We just assume that we can
unload all of our weight on them
and since some college gave them
a piece of paper with fancy writing on it
it solidified that they were also bodybuilders

That's the same thing we do
to our strong friends.
We hand them our endless baggage,
and since you've never seen
them in a moment of weakness
or since they've never allowed you to see
that sometimes they break down and cry too,
that they must always be able
to carry the world on their backs.

Check on your strong friend.

20 Something

Somewhere along the way I made the mistake,

of thinking 20 something came with endless expiration dates.

I always thought by 20 something, I had to have it all down and figured out.

I had to have this, be here, achieve that, before it was too late,

as if I was running late for destiny's date and stuck in traffic on my way to a meeting with my fate

I thought I had to know instead of grow, and be there already instead of on the way,

but nobody told me that my 20 somethings would be like a GPS that chose to reroute every year or two along the way.

20 something is for mistakes made and friends gained, instead of superficial dreams filled with predictability,

 while your true passion withers away and dies slowly

20 something isn't for rushing to bloom as much as the appreciation of growing, because no two flowers will ever possess the same petals

20 something is for me, but I spent a part looking for a "we" filled potential and things we thought we'd be.

when all along maybe 20 something was never meant to come with a passenger seat.

20 something is the mirror showing you who you truly are but also reflects who you aspire to be

It's a time of humility, for transition,

a time to understand yourself before you can ever get another.

And although I learned to walk long ago, 20 something seems to be when my feet matter to me the most.

I want 20 something to host the journey towards a destination that is meant for me to truly be happy,

so please excuse me if I'm a bit more selfish for a little while longer, and I'll never ask for anything other than patience,

because 20 something is for me.

Cry Alone

I've always preferred to suffer in private,

where everything's quiet.

Where I don't have to answer questions,

about why I'm temporarily overlooking my blessings.

When things get tough, instead of externally explode

I choose to not tell another soul.

For me, it's always been easier to cry alone

The Rain

I recently noticed that some birds
sing the most beautiful songs
while it's raining.
We should all be like those birds,
even in the most adverse weather,
when everything around us looks unfavorable
we find a reason to sing

Black Mother in America

Being a black mother in America
has to be terrifying.
You create something so great,
but all too often
you have to give it back entirely too soon

Prisons Are The New Plantations

It's been a while since we were in those fields doing master's job for free, while we did the labor they collected the wealth that our ancestors would never see.

Oppressed to the point where many would rather risk their lives and try to flee

Hundreds of years later we're living under the impression that we are free but if you take a step back and view our society in its entirety you'll see

We live in a place where our people are hurt, and the main reason is others have been able to determine our worth.

Our children grow up thinking the only way out is a jump shot or crack rock, so when they go to school they never see it as a useful tool

And while they're not learning, the government is earning, and they want more because they build prisons based off third grade test scores

Handcuffs are the new noose, and our people are crammed in jail with no proof making all the things for all the stores you give your money to

So you can act like you don't see it, but I do...

Prisons are the new plantations.

Black Roses

A rose was never supposed to grow here.

Cracked concrete was never meant to birth such a majestic seed misplaced and forced to bloom regardless of its forgotten roots

Pushing through the hard pavement of a past meant to prevent anything from ever rising above it.

Deprived from what it really needs by lack of protection and poverty,

water coming only from the rainy days that it was able to barely sustain with petals sun dried and drained, but this rose still stands & remains.

No matter how many roses before this one were clipped and put in a box or vase to wither away

No matter what other roses died from doubt, & failure with potential put on pause by life's flaws.

No matter if it was the only rose that seemed to grow and stand alone on lonely roads traveled by few.

A rose was never meant to grow here,

but somewhere in the concrete, a rose is growing anyway

Skydive

When you look like me
an extreme sport is walking down the street
that's why we don't waste time
learning how to surf and ski

As soon as my feet touch
the concrete outside of my front door
a target a mile wide
appears on the front and back of me

When you look like me,
a trip to Walmart or the park
never comes with a guarantee
that I'll make it back alive to my family

That's why I never had the luxury of snowboarding.

Because when you look like me
getting pulled over is extreme enough for me
so a NASCAR race is something I never needed to see.

So when they ask me
why I have no desire to try any
of these things, a smile spreads across my face
and I say "When you're a black man, you skydive every
day."

Just Be Friends

We can't just be friends
after what we originally
tried to be ended
with both of our hearts distant
and we placed each other
back at the beginning
like nothing ever happened

If we can't be public lovers
I'd rather us be public strangers
because what I can't do
is go from looking at you
as part of the blueprint
of my future, to looking at you
like we never shared a past.
I can't act like we're not trying
to turn a part of both of our movies
into deleted scenes and put on
a façade of a false friendship.

And I can't look at you like I haven't seen
you undressed down to your last insecurity.

I can't unfeel what was felt
and use a platonic band aid
to cover up a stab wound
to the chest that Cupid had every intention
of landing in our hearts
but we both seemed to flinch

at the last minute causing
our target to be missed

So I can't say that we
can just be friends
because in the back of
both of our minds
before we close our eyes at night
in separate beds, we'll
find ourselves wondering
about what more we could've been.

Recording Kindness

Stop taking all the nobility
out of your random acts of kindness
by recording them for everyone to see.

Friend

If I call you my friend
that comes with a lifetime warranty
and loyalty that amounts to every
grain of sand on the beach.
Time nor distance will never be
the reason to ever bring an end to
how much I cherish you.
I don't care if it's been 50 years
and an ocean kept us thousands of miles apart,
if I ever call you my friend,
that's something that not even death could end.
Because to me, friend is synonymous with kin
so a friend to me, will always be family.

Learning Curve

You should take every relationship
that you've ever been in
and figure out every part
that was meant to be a lesson learned

It's extremely disrespectful
to present the same carbon copy
of yourself relationship after relationship
without any improvements made
to be a better edition of yourself
for the next person that
chooses to invest themselves in you

Change

The only way things won't
remain the same,
is if we change.
But if we never change,
how can we ever complain?
How can we say, with
a straight face, that
we really want change
when we've failed
to first change ourselves?

Writing On the Wall

The writing on the wall,
is never a lie.
You'll never read a fairytale
where a tragedy resides

A Misguided Man's Dream

I think I've already met the woman I'm supposed to be with...

I don't know if we know each other extremely well or just in passing yet, but I think I've met her

But the problem isn't in me not knowing her, it's in meeting the me that I'm supposed to be before time turns her eyes towards another man

My past includes great women that I'll never have a bad thing to ever utter a word about because I know the reason we deferred and didn't work out...was me

Too caught in the insecurity of giving all of me to the point she was left with nothing.

nothing left to hold on to, nothing to no longer make this blurred reality a mirage of fairytales ending happily ever after, even though she knew ahead resided a beautiful disaster

Keeping them arm's length away so at least that was close enough to feel my touch but whenever steps seemed to be taken forward for a full embrace I would always choose to step away

See I've never seen love work firsthand..

I've never seen what it's like to work through the arguments and fights and know that things would be alright in the morning

I've never seen love be given unconditionally from a man to a woman to the point where his pride and male ego was set aside and let his guard down until all of him would reside inside her hands

So all I ask from whoever's next, whoever's left, whoever's not afraid of a good hearted man with intentions to do right that was just given a misguided plan...

While I figure this out...

Please, be patient with me

Hold My Hand

Sometimes all I need
is for you to hold my hand.
You don't have to say a word,
just put your hand inside of mine
and don't let go

Reciprocate

I think that some white people
operate out of the fear
of black people wanting to do to them,
what was first done onto them

I also think that there are
some black people that operate
out of the anger to reciprocate
the hate that they first felt

Both are equally wrong.

The goal should never be
dominance or authority,
but death to power
by the way of empathy

Heaven

Heaven ain't a place
with streets paved with gold
it's that feeling you get
when you inflict a smile
across the face of somebody
you care for

It ain't a place with angels
or flower filled pastures
but the sound of genuine laughter
that you let leave your lungs

Heaven ain't a place in the sky
that you earn your way to
if you do everything right,
but it's when you decide
in your heart is where love
and happiness resides

Heaven was never a place,
it was always a state of mind.

Hell

Hell ain't a place
where impure souls burn in a fiery lake,
it's where heartache from grave mistakes
make us internally debate
whether or not we deserve another chance.

It ain't a place God sends us
forever to think about mistakes,
it's how we feel after we get burned
by lessons we should've already learned

Hell ain't a place in the ground
where second chances are never allowed,
it's the place the voice in your head
takes you with every echo of
"I'm not good enough."

Hell ain't a mythical dreaded place
it's where our inferior state
of mind resides.

Read Me

One day, whoever I end up being with,

I'll give her this notebook with all this shit in it, and
leave the room until she's read it all and finished.

She always said I was so closed off and I never talked
to her as much as I should, but little did she know

my soul was enclosed right inside of this book.

I'll let her read about every muse that I ever used and
never shared,

let her read my candid memories and examine
everything that ever motivated words and moved me
to care.

The endless lines written about my self-doubt and
the things I wish I could change,

where my perception and my reflection weren't
synonymous and my mistakes wouldn't allow me to
see my own gains.

Chapters about lessons learned from every woman
that was before her,

exposing all my flaws that others saw hoping that
what she witnessed wouldn't be reason for our
downfall.

My imperfections put into words,

from every noun written down to every verb my pen
produced that my soul overheard.

Giving her the ability to judge me completely,

with hopes that instead she'll choose not to and
continue to love me unconditionally,

even though she flipped through endless lines made
into rhymes of my very own history.

But there's a catch, I can only do this one time.

The idea of letting my unedited life be seen by eyes
other than mine already bears a heavy price, so I
could never imagine allowing myself to do it twice.

So hopefully I choose right.

And whoever it is that's meant to see my life written
is meant to be with me forever whenever I decide.

Choosing instead to climb this mountain of words
I've built for my own protection, instead of letting it
scare her in another direction.

Or maybe, it'll never happen at all.

Maybe my words were never meant to be shared, and maybe I'm a fool to be fooled into thinking someone else really cared.

So if it just so happens I never build a union strong enough to equate the amount of trust I'll truly need,

and this autobiography holding my wildest thoughts merged with my most complex dreams will remain unseen,

so be it.

But until then,

I'll continue to write like the only people that'll ever read, are you and me.

When My Ancestors Built America

The American dream never included me,
but instead thrived off my demise.
But the irony is,
America was built
by hands that resembled mine.
Sweat trickled down a black face
that looked like mine.
Whips whipped across a black back
that looked like mine.
Chains chained black feet
of a man that resembled me,
as he built the very place
he'd never be free to live peacefully

Time

Time told our story
better than either one of us ever could.

In 50 Years

We'll be old and grey haired
swaying peacefully in rocking chairs
wrinkly skinned and surrounded by grandchildren,

and they'll ask you about your life.
How will you reply?

Will they be descendants of a dreamer,
or a soul that let complacency take control?

A person that lived a life worth imitation,
or someone that lived in fear and procrastination?

A world traveling, humanity loving individual,
or a story filled with unreached potential?

What will you say?

Can you say you treated others the right way,
and leaned to find beauty in flaws and mistakes,

or lived a life of bitterness?

When you look at your grandkids,
will you really be able say
that you lived?

Famous

I might sound selfish for saying this,
but I hope you're never famous.
I hope that to so many others you remain nameless
and anonymous in the eyes of strangers.
I don't want them to see you,
to love you, to adore you
the way that I do.
I hope they never put you on a pedestal
because if they do
my biggest fear on the ground,
is I'll get lost in the crowd.

Melting Pot

For the people that believe
that America is a melting pot,
why don't I seem to blend in
when I walk into a bank for a loan?
Why am I made to feel so out of place
around a bunch of people
with a different colored face?
Why do I stand out in every store I visit
when my skin is accused of shoplifting
before it can make a purchase?
Why is it so hard for me to go unnoticed
while I'm having a family BBQ
or at the swimming pool
or selling water on my porch
for a buck or two?
Why is my existence used as your cue
to call police in hopes of my body
morphing into a bloody hashtag
in the middle of the street?

If America is such a melting pot,
why do I continue to get treated so separately?

The Part I Hate

Don't tell me
we went through all of this together
just to act like strangers
years from now
when we're in the same room.

Welcome to America

where soda is more harmful than marijuana,
yet nobody's ever been to prison for a Pepsi.

God Is A Black Woman

I met God last night
and She was black.
Her hair thick and dark
like the midnight July sky
Her skin as soft as springtime rain
and her touch felt like every breeze
that came just in time.
Her voice mimicked melodies
only heard from birds
that knew what heaven
looked like firsthand
Her eyes held hands
with the clouds and
her lips were full enough
to make oceans mere pools
Her hips curved like the Nile
and housed life with every sway
with a smile that the sun
tried to imitate daily

But what's crazy is,
I don't think She has a clue
She might not realize
that what the world
told her wasn't beautiful
they then try to emulate
from her hair to her shape
to every feature featured on her face.
She might not see that

the world resides in her palms
no matter how hard they tried
to convince her that she wasn't invincible
Convince her that the origin of life
on this Earth didn't first
derive from between her own thighs

We don't exist without you
you beautiful black God
whose steps should be worshipped
and name should be held
in highest regards when spoken.

You are the epitome,
of what God is.

Worst Enemy

Maybe, it's not the world
that's holding you back
maybe it's you
that hand stitched the straight jacket
in which you reside

How long will you continue to be
your own worst enemy?

Mamma's Voice

I hear my mamma's voice in my head
every time things get hard
I hear her telling me
all the things she used to say
when I was younger
that she thought I wasn't listening to,
I heard every word.

My Last Day

I want the day that I stop learning
to be the day that I start living
The day I ignore the benefit in my mistakes
and choose to use ignorance
as my guiding direction
Continuing to chase perfection in reality
instead of making my reality perfection
I want my last day to be when I
no longer recognize blessings

I want the day to stop loving
to be the day I stop living,
when no empathy is left inside of me
and I'm no longer capable of giving.
Even when it hurts to give,
even when you have every reason
to take, but wonder instead
how much you have left in the end
When I'm empty, let that be the end of me

The day I can no longer make
this world a better place
when every piece of love and laughter
I have left leaves me and my eyes
can no longer warm another's face,
I want that to be my last day.

Let me outlive my fears and heartbroken tears
soaked into my pillows over years,

let me live to see the best accomplishments
of family and closest friends
Let my life come to an end
the day I've done everything on this journey
and it's time for a new one to begin.

Skin

Its far deeper than skin

and most are pretty pennies.

On the outside, shiny and new

but no value internally.

You know my first layer perfectly,

every scar and blemish on my skin.

But a stranger to every layer within.

So even undressed right in front of you,

to the wrong one my soul is unrecognizable.

Insanity

Somebody has to say something different,
if not we'll remain in the same position.
Same routine expecting different results
will always leave us thinking
that something's missing.
Until we classify our women
as queens instead of bitches
and our kings are no longer just niggas,
we'll always be our own worst enemies.

The definition of insanity.

Somebody's gotta do something different.
Chasing money can't be the only commitment,
but as long as it is,
we'll continue to do whatever we have to
in order to get it.

Somebody's gotta tell them,
that knowledge matters
or we'll always be at the bottom of the ladder
looking up.

Even though every tool is in our possession
to end our own regression,

but we must be insane.

To Every Crush I've Ever Had

I like you.
I like you like sleeping in on a Saturday
and like reaching in my pocket
and finding exact change.
I like you like clothes fresh out the dryer,
like that interview I killed and found out
that I was hired.

I like you,
like when I order 10 wings and get 11,
like sunshine in the springtime
when I feel parallel to heaven.
I like you like I like to look at you,
when I know that you're not staring
like the end of my shift on Friday
when I'm no longer caring

I like you like Alfalfa liked Darla,
like when something good happens
in the form of returned karma.
I like you like flies like summertime BBQs
like climbing mountaintops and looking down
on my problems from a different view

24

I ignore you to protect you,
from a man lost in his own soul.
Instead of telling what sounds good
without genuine intent,
I'd rather not say anything

Scars

Scars are the body's story of the soul

Scars are the memories

of times of brokenness,

times when I left my flesh exposed.

These scars remind me,

that I once felt pain

and eventually found a way to heal

Let You Go

Before I love you wrong
I'll let you go.
Before I stifle your growth,
I'll remove my shadow.
Before I'm unworthy
to keep holding your hand,
I'll keep mine closed.
Instead of just something
if I'm incapable of being your everything,
 I'd rather be nothing
Before I'm no longer your peace
 right before you fall asleep,
 I'd rather be your forgotten dream.
 Before I'm no longer the answer,
 I'd rather not be a possibility.
 And before I overstay my welcome,
 I'll excuse myself early.

One Way Love

I only know how to love one way,
so I had to learn how to love less.
Or I'd end up giving all of my love away.
Either I love you completely,
or not at all.

But what I don't need,
is another halfway love
because every piece of me
given to another one
is a piece less left I have
to offer the next.

Pillow Talk

Talk to me, and tell me everything.
Tell me all the ways that they
did it wrong, so that I won't.
So I can stop this from being
a repeat of another sad song.

You inhibitions will never leave this room
no matter if you feel like it's too soon
and apprehension collides with your intuition
leaving you conflicted about what to do.
the secrets that you confide in me
will never be between another
other than me and you.

These pillows hold all your truth
and treats every single insecurity you
confessed like precious jewels.
 These pillows are the unguarded mind's diary
listening to everything,
but never repeating anything

3:36 PM

A place where they kill all of your leaders,
and then point out how lost you are

Don't Lie

Whatever you do, just don't lie

The words might be hard to find,

the timing may never be perfect,

but for what it's worth,

don't lie.

Even if it may be the last thing

I wanna hear,

and it confirms my biggest fear,

even if the truth comes

coupled with tears,

a lie is the last thing I desire to hear.

With the truth you can eventually heal,

but lies always leave an open wound.

So no matter what mistakes are made

and what you do, I'd rather hear the truth.

Love It All

Learn to love it all,

not only the fortunate times

but as well the times you fall.

Change

Don't be afraid to change,

never were we supposed

to always remain exactly the same.

Grow every chance given,

one day your limbs will reach their peak.

Do you want to be fragile

with roots that are weak

or in a crowded forest

one of the tallest trees?

O.W.E.

It's hard for a prince to become king

when there's first no king

to teach him anything.

An heiress can never become queen

when queens are chasing misguided dreams.

The last thing we can continue to be,

are our own worst enemies.

Our children need to see,

that their skin comes without boundaries,

but that starts with you and me.

Lifeline

The people closest to me always say

that I should pick up the phone more

and I always promise that I will.

But somewhere in between becoming

a man and consuming myself with my dreams,

I always get lost in life.

My call log is mostly incoming calls,

but the irony is that the same people

I pray for daily hardly hear from me at all.

Wondering if I'm okay,

and I always tell them I'm straight

regardless of how many times life

leads me in crooked lines.

Keeping all of me to myself,

while all they want is conversation and time.

Replacing memories made with ones

that mean the most spending time chasing myself

never acknowledging that help

is always only a call away.

But the relationships I put on the highest shelves

are the ones I reach for the least

But no matter how things may be,

I need you to know that once I love you

I love you unconditionally.

I know my ways may make it seem

like you mean nothing,

but to me you mean more than anything

Hopefully one day I'll find a way to

show it better in the physical

and not solely based on my heart's intent.

Hopefully I won't pick up the phone

only to find that I became

my own lifeline

Lived Backwards

Life might be lived backwards,

maybe at birth we know everything we need

and we begin to lose it all

the longer we live.

We know love but we learn hate,

the exact same way

we often know better

but instead choose

to learn through mistakes.

It could be a chance that maybe,

life was meant to be lived

looking from the other way

Only Yours

I want your eyes to be

the only ones able to read my story.

Your eyes are the only ones I trust,

to not let it scare you away.

No matter what chapters leave me drenched

in my own shame with nobody left to blame.

No matter how many pages are stuck together

by memories I tried to forget forever,

you'll find a way to separate every page.

My trust within another other than myself

with these things, only resides in you.

With me, I only trust you.

Only your eyes have what it takes

to make it down every page.

Her

Something about a woman.
A woman that doesn't need
a man to be her validity.
A woman so in touch with herself,
that her touch fills voids with ease.
The way she smells,
like invisible roses chose her crown
as their home.
The way she walks,
putting a pause on the room
as she continues to move,
her soul's essence leaving a trail
of the sweetest perfume.
A woman who holds the world
in her palm and your future in her eyes,
penetrating every lie that you told yourself
to be convinced that a God doesn't exist.
Until she proves to be firsthand proof of this.

Time

It's funny that when I look at the clock now,

it seems to move faster than it did

when I was a kid.

A week is the new month and New Year's Eve

seems to get here a little quicker every time.

And no matter what we would do over,

we're never given the option to rewind.

But if we could fast forward

when we were kids,

we would have never been

in such a rush to grow up

and race with time.

Falling

Falling for you was never the hard part,
but staying on the ground is where
I seemed to have the most trouble.
I never allowed myself to ever feel
grounded in anybody else.
No matter if they had the capability
of being exactly what I would need,
I had a bad habit of turning forever
into a season.
Even for reasons at times
I could never explain.

No Role Models

The kids ain't got role models,
just people being glorified
for all the wrong reasons,
for all the things
they should never wanna be.
The kids ain't got no direction
but neither do we.
Because if we did,
so would they.
As the sun turns,
we stay in place
and the kids see it all,
until our norms are theirs
and our decisions
become their living.

Nothing New

Ain't nothing on the news but the blues,

and the soul is wearing tattered clothes

but the shoes are new.

Appealing to the eye,

all the while rotting inside.

You always feed the soul

whether you know it or not

but the problem is

while smiles are warm

hearts become cold

and what used to be gold

now resembles coal.

Land of The Free

If you really think that this
is the land of the free
you may be part of the problem
instead of the possibility.
How can we be free
when the land was ours initially,
and the real natives in their own home
were forced into slavery?
How can we be free,
when saying "I can't breathe"
falls on deaf ears?
How can we really be free,
in a place that hates the skin
I was born in
and my biggest fear is being
a black man that lives here?
Every time I turn on the TV
someone else that looks just like me
is killed by police.
Philando. Eric. Mike. Alton.
They were me.
Sons that never got to tell
their mothers again that they love 'em.
Fathers that were stolen
from sons and daughters forever,
and husbands that never told wives
being black would cost them their lives
as they read eulogies of their lovers

with tear filled eyes.
So when people tell me,
that we live in the land of the free,
you'll have to excuse me
if I see things differently.

The Mis-educated Definition of A Man

Man up.
Stand up.
And face life with your hands up
and clenched fists
ready to show your strength.
Poke your chest out
and keep your head high,
don't listen when they
tell you weakness is okay,
it's only a state of mind.
Your eyes should never meet tears,
even when looking your fears
in the face,
but then again
you should never have fears anyway.
Compassion and openness,
that ain't you,
to be a man means
your emotions remain hidden
and only give them
what the outside can see.
Be colder than this cold world
that you were born into,
that's what men do.
And I don't care
if you're left with the weight
of the world to shoulder
and bear, find a way

to lift it anyway.
And make sure that you
don't exhibit the slightest
grimace or strain.
A real man,
always hides his pain.
Build a fortress with walls
that stretch to the heavens
secure enough to handle
the blows of your life's
most deadliest weapons,
and no matter what you do
never ever let anyone in.
No matter how bad you want to,
not even a woman
or closest friends.
To be a real man,
means knowing how to isolate
and never take vulnerability
on a blind date.

Settle Down

I'm starting to think,
that settling down with another
is no longer the thing for me.
Not because I'm still running streets,
but when I do think that finally
I've found someone that gets it,
that gets me,
they always find a way
to show me how difficult
loving me can possibly be.
I've had backs turned in my face,
and affirming smiles replaced
by the uncertainty from those
I thought were there to stay.
I've slept in the bed,
with memories impersonating lovers,
and shared covers with women
that swore they were so different
from all the others.
But in my case,
they've all ended up the same.
Vowing to always be my tomorrows,
but never staying around
and ending up
as just another yesterday.

Pro Black

Don't ever let them tell you,

that pro black and anti-white are the same.

Just because you learned to love your skin,

never means that you learned to hate them.

Pro black means that you know better

than to be seen as just 3/5 of a person.

Bad Days

I've never seen a day so bad

that the sun decided

to sit the next one out.

Either Or

Either love me, or leave me alone.

But what you won't do is continue to highlight my
imperfections while you white out my efforts.

When I'm giving you the best of me, only to feel like
my shots at your heart constantly miss their mark

And I start to contemplate if what we have is worth
the wait,

or should I let it go.

Bullets 'n School

Since when, did sending your kids to school turn you into a murder accessory?

22 times this year alone, bullets have entered classrooms and turned schools into memorials.

Kids learning to read and write with the rest of their lives left to live never knew that today,

their dreams would end in the same place that dreams are supposed to be cultivated and made

22 times mothers left their kids after breakfast and didn't know they wouldn't be able to make it to dinner

22 times kids never knew that in the middle of math lessons would halt to shattering glass as screams rang out from hallways that were safe yesterday

22 times kids were sent to school in hopes of finding their way, but instead ran in to a dead end that resembled automatic weapons.

Revolvers revolving in the very place where the only thing revolving was supposed to be minds and thoughts from the things being taught.

Who knew, that sending your kids to school, would sign them up for a premature funeral?

Holes

These holes that I have, need to be filled

But not be anyone else, except myself.

Because if I allow another to fill my voids,

if they ever must go,

I'll be filled with holes again.

Fine Print

They say that it takes 21 consecutive days to form a habit,

eventually it merges itself into your life and becomes second nature to the point that you no longer have to remind yourself to do it.

But breaking a habit is totally different.

It can take anywhere from a day to never, and while some have the courage to quit cold turkey, others gently rock themselves to ease in their own comfort and conformity

Unaware, that a contract they signed with their own time after 21 days, came with a lifetime lease.

Always read the fine print

When They Ask About Us

I hope that when they ask you about us, you decide to tell them the truth.

Instead of painting me with broad strokes of negativity, find it in yourself to tell them what really happened to our incomplete masterpiece

Tell them that I was a good man, although my blemishes and imperfections did exist, let everyone know that you were so fixated on them you never cared to stare at the big picture.

Tell them about how I tried to handle your heart like my most valuable possession, but my worth never quite amounted to your expectations no matter how much change I tried to add.

But if you'd be honest with them, and yourself, you'd say that my bad couldn't outweigh my good on its heaviest day.

Tell them that I was ready to love you in more ways than stars in the sky, but you always seemed to want clouds on clear nights.

Strong Grip

I've always found it ironic

that I have such a strong grip,

but a bad habit of letting go way too easily.

When I feel that what I'm holding wants to be free,

I help it out by separating my fingers,

 and watching it leave.

Asylum

At times my mind resembles an asylum,

padded walls to keep my insecurities in check,

a strait jacket to keep my ideas from killing
themselves,

and a resident therapist that never seems quite
qualified to offer the perfect remedy.

Passion's Interlude

When I lay with you all I hear is music..

Like tight rhymes over a perfect beat our hearts pound in synchrony,

the treble of your voice as you tremble serves as the perfect harmony for our passion's instrumental.

Moans mimicking melodies and the bass from my voice bounce off every wall you possess as we create such a beautiful mess.

Let's write lyrics with subtle touches from fingertips that turn into tight grips as crescendos from repeated climax echo the perfect pitch.

The rhythm of deep breaths coming from our chests dance around each other as late night turns to sunrise and our duet demands one more curtain call.

And we both know our song is one that can never be created with another,

and the evidence is in the way that our souls made perfect music with one other

Return To Sender

The world has a strange way of taking everything we give to it,

and delivering it right back to our doorstep.

Always be mindful of what you send,

it'll be back soon.

Creator

I find it hard to believe,
that from the hands of a man
came so much beauty

I believe to be a creator
you have to have traits
that make it possible to create

Give a woman a house,
and she creates a home

Give a woman a seed,
she creates a life

Give a woman anything,
and she creates reciprocity

So how can I believe,
that a man would be responsible
for all the things I see?

Intentions

Live with the awareness
that you're always on stage
for the world to see,
but act as if the room is empty
when you perform.

Lab Rat

All of my siblings are either engaged or married,
and I'm the oldest of five

I wonder if the reason their road to a happy home
seems to be shorter than mine,
is due to the fact that they saw me
ruin love so much, they knew
exactly what not to do.

They saw me repeatedly
with what seemed to be love in the palm of my hands,
and I made the decision
to no longer hold on to anything.

And silently, they learned from me the lesson
of abusing blessings and figured out alternate
directions to take before making the mistake
of having love right in front of your face,
and watching it walk away.

And since there was nobody to teach me,
I had to learn all these things the hard way,
while they had front row seats
to every single one of my mistakes.

Buy Back The Block

I wake up in apartment 3B,

and it's the first of the month

which means it's time to come outta pocket

and pay the fee for living to somebody that

looks nothing like me.

This building is full of blacks, but not a single

one owns the rights to their own homes so

really we're building Little Chinatown

while the ones a little darker brown pay rent

and don't have 2 pennies to rub together in

the end.

I walk down the street to get something to eat,

and every restaurant I see is owned by

nobody that looks like me.

But Korean and Japanese food floods the streets

of all the people that look just like me.

And even if I wanted to buy groceries,

the Arab supermarket is the only place on my

block that I can shop.

Chinese selling my sisters Indian weaves to

imitate false European ideals and dreams

and I can't seem to understand how every

other race knows the pulse of our supply and

demand so well except for us.

Why is it that to be black on my block means

my welfare comes from people that

don't look like me?

That don't care about me?

That would find another black block

to rebuild and sell these same things if we died
overnight.

And why,

why do we continue to allow our

neighborhoods to turn into their venues

as we continue to throw every dollar we

struggled to make back into hands that don't

give a damn about our race?

If our people ever wanna see the light of day

and take back what was taken away,

even though we built with our bare hands most

of the buildings that we don't own today,

the only way, is to buy back the block.

Bleeding Out

When a heart breaks, it never breaks even.

And you walked away with the bigger piece,

leaving me to hold onto fractions

of what used to be complete.

They say time heals all wounds,

but time must've forgot about this one.

The red stream that runs to the floor,

has never had a chance to dry.

Hoping that time keeps it's end

of the bargain, and keeps me

from bleeding out.

In You

I swear I was outside last night,
and when I looked up somehow the stars
were spelling out your name.

There was a butterfly I saw the other day
that I swear carried your scent in its wings
as it flew away.

I went to the beach recently,
and for a second while I sat there quietly
I swear I heard your voice in the melody
of the waves.

I think what I'm trying to say is
that in my mind everything synonyms
with what I think is beautiful,

I made synonymous with the idea you

Your smile is like perfect scenery and good lighting,
your walk is like a perfect breeze,
and your presence is the essence
of God's prized possession manifested
in human form

Your eyes turn into a vacation that ends too soon,
your touch is an alarm clock that makes sleeping in
an afterthought.

So I think what I'm trying to say is,
in you is where I find everything
that I ever felt in my life
was beautiful.

Reminisce

It's on nights like this,
where I'm stuck between
if I wanna reminisce,
or do I want our memories
from the past to be the only
thing we can't remember.

So do we really need to create
something new, or now that
we've moved on and are comfortable
do we have to revisit the past?

Racist Reminders

20 minutes away from my house,
confederate flags still occupy front yards
and reside on the tallest flagpole
plantation money could buy.

So how do we tell black folks
to get over slavery
when the very culprits
remind us of it daily?

Withdrawal

I've always found it odd,
that former alcoholics die when
they're older, not from drinking
but from symptoms of withdrawal

That taught me to never make
something I choose to live with now
turn into something I can't
live without later.

#1

Your peace should always be your main priority.

Only Real Religion

To treat every woman
as the mother of God.
To treat every man
as the reflection of God.
To treat every child
as the child of God.

This is the only religion,
we were designed to live by.

12:09 AM

My two closest friends,
are my reflection and my shadow.

But one has a terrible memory
and can never quite recognize me
when we run into one another,
and the other always finds a way
to disappear when I'm in the dark.

Star Gazing

You can go outside tonight,
look up and see the sky hosting
countless stars that we can all
see at the exact same time in
the exact same place.
Yet it's humanly impossible to travel to a star,
to the point where you'd live and die over 1,000 times
before you made it to any of them.

I wonder if this is the reason I look at things that
seem out of reach, and decide they're unattainable
before I ever begin to journey towards them

Maybe that's why I felt like I never deserved you,
you were the brightest star in the sky
and who was I to be so lucky
to call it mine?

Why I Became a Vegan

In a world that's already designed
to kill me, the least I can do
is not help them.

Tying Shoes

I wanna learn to love you
the same way I learned
how to tie my shoes.

Practicing all day,
each time getting a little closer
until it was finally perfect
and once I figured it out
I never forgot how to again

The Definition

If you look up the word love
in the dictionary, its defined as
an intense feeling of deep affection.

I asked a 6 year old what love was,
she said it's when you hug someone
even when they make you angry.

Kids have a funny way of
making things make sense,
because I spent so much time
treating love like an equation
instead of my own handwritten story.

It was never meant to have one solution,
but the possibility of infinite endings

Fear Death

When people ask me why I don't fear death,
I ask them what's the benefit
in being scared of something
that's guaranteed to occur
regardless of how I feel about it

Be Safe

The fact that out of habit
I end every conversation
with every black man I talk to
with the words "be safe"
comes from living in a place
where you can go from
father, husband, or son
to a hashtag and eulogy
with a trip to the gas station.

Insecure

The insecurity ruined everything.

But in the beginning, it felt like the potential for
wedding rings,

    just like it always starts off to seem.

It was genuine and consistency was there
consistently,

    texts were never left unreplied to or unread and
calls were answered before it could ring,

    everything was everything.

But one day, for some reason it changed,

    and ironically it was around the same time feelings
seemed to finally become fully exchanged.

After doing everything to get her, suddenly it seemed
as if his intentions began to differ.

She used to feel like the answer, and now he made
her heart feel more like an option.

That energy was replaced with empty space that
used to be occupied with perfect chemistry,

but instead now is the residence of insecurity.

"Their" time turned into "his" time, where it was always okay to communicate when she was the one on his mind.

But if the tables ever turned the minute she acted like she wasn't with it she got accused of being uncommitted,

all for giving him a dose of his own medicine.

Every conversation turned into an insecurity demonstration,

where trust was shown at an all-time low, and every sentence ended with uncertainty.

And certainly he knew what he was doing,

using his own insecure ways to flip the script on her and manipulate.

Telling her all the ways she was doing it wrong when it was him that lacked all along,

but he knew that if he made her feel this way, like she was the one on the wrong page,

like she wasn't the one living up to her end of the wage,

it would buy him time if she chose to stay.

But little did he know that she peeped game, and cried her last tear over him and them yesterday.

Tired of her feelings feeling inferior, she examined her interior only to find

that insecurities were taking place of her peace of mind,

and what she once felt was a fairytale now resembled a land mine.

So it was in her best interest to escape while there was still time.

And before she packed and left it all behind she left with him this simple line:

"The insecurity that killed our shared dream,

came from never making yourself feel secure in me."

Wednesday

Some days, I don't wanna write
even though I know
that I should.
Even though I constantly
feel as if my soul
will explode,
if I fail to turn these
feelings into dry ink.
Even when I don't know
how I feel, or think some
things are better left unwritten.
Some days, it's hard to
share these feelings
even with myself,
because most don't know
that writers tend to have
a bad habit of letting their
words serve as their therapist
and some days I'd rather not
be a client on my own sofa.
But what happens is
that these seas of similes
and mountains of metaphors
become a barrier between me
and my very own peace.
Sometimes I try to suppress my pen
to keep from bleeding out
without knowing what part of me
will remain mine

because for every blank page
an artist gives life to
in return a part of them dies.

Date w/ Potential

She sat by the door
staring at the time nervously
and tapping her foot
to the rhythm of every second

She saw others enter the same door
I told her I was 5 minutes away from
an hour ago.

But growing all too familiar
with the feeling of me standing her up
she calmly gathered her stuff
and left.

In search of somebody
she wouldn't have to keep
waiting forever for.

Memoirs of An Absentee Father

I think my father is a good man
that made some bad decisions,
I never really knew him,
but I've seen him a few times.
We lived in the same small town
but I've never been to his house.
All of the visits were brief,
and our relationship never left the surface.
Everything about being a man
I had to teach myself,
while he chose to form a separate family
that never included me.

I don't hate you
but I can't say that I love you either,
and even though we share identical features
to me you were always a stranger.
But the worst part about not knowing you
is it left a piece of me unrecognizable.
It's so much about me I struggle with
that maybe you had answers to
but instead, I stumbled my way through
and still became a man without you.

And I don't hate you,
but I can't say I love you either,
and I'll never blame you again
for anything I might go through,
but some days it's so hard not to.

A Fifth of "If"

If "if" was a fifth,
make sure you're not the one
that had one too many
due to shots filled
with unfulfilled possibility.

Be the sober friend
with the keys
that always wants to go home early.

Dear Black Boy

Dear black boy,

I've dreaded the day that I'd have to sit you down and have this conversation.

I've dreaded the very day that your pure soul became tainted by this corrupt world and you didn't understand why you were being judged by what you were instead of who you were.

I've dreaded the day that you discovered the world wasn't colorblind.

I know that innocence lost is never retained..

So even now as I write these words it hurts me to think that every conversation you have with another black boy will eventually end with the words "be safe."

It hurts me to think that a routine traffic stop or going to the park to play could turn into your premature judgement day.

Dear black boy,

please understand that there was a reason they were scared for us to know how to read and intentionally broke apart our families, a reason why they'll hire you for manual labor but won't tell you in order for you to be completely free you have to be the CEO of your own company

You were meant to be the king of so much more than just the streets and most things that come on tv are exactly what they want you to see and aspire to be...

nothing.

You can do so much more than dribble a ball and sing a song, this whole country was built on the backs of the people that look just like you and me

Dear black boy,

Don't ever limit your dreams

You'll have to be twice as good, twice as punctual, twice as educated just in order to be half considered so be three times, no five times, no ten times as thorough in everything that you choose to do.

Don't fight hate with hate despite what some may say around you, even a lot of our own people...

because regardless of race, hate and love don't always have color, and if it did we wouldn't kill each other

Love your brother regardless of a mutual mother because now more than ever, we all need each other

Dear black boy,

Be strong, be smart, follow the brightest path you can choose

But dear black boy,

Out of everything you do, be the best black man you can be, I promise it's possible.

Lyin' King

Whoever came up with the
phrase "the heart doesn't lie"
has clearly never been in love
only to see it not work out,
because mine has deceived me
a few times.

Martin's Demise

They didn't touch Martin
when he was having a dream
and fighting for integration,
but when he realized that all
this time, he was leading his people
into a burning nation

Seeds

Every living thing first starts as a seed,
from people to trees,
we're all just the contents
of what was once
the inside of a seed

One day, we were nothing
and our being didn't exist
until our seed decided
that what was inside it
they needed the world to see.

No Label

When you take away the labels
and strip all the status
what does your bare soul
bring to the table?

When all the designer on your
back and feet become obsolete
and your soul is left naked
for the world to see,
what exactly will be seen?

Will we see a soul
that still glows
like the rarest of jewels,
or will we see somebody
with no value to show
because all of the their worth
was only externally
placed on things
that we can see and show.

Hopefully your soul,
looks just as good naked
as it does in nice clothes.

10:21 PM

Life is finding peace
from getting less
of what you want
and more of what you need

Help Wanted

At times my life feels like a store
with a huge "Help Wanted" sign
plastered in the window
for the world to see
looking to employ anybody willing
to restock the happiness
and sweep the floor clean
of all the doubt that my insecurities
left a lingering trail of,
register my sanity to make sure
correct change is always made
for my mistakes.
Dust the shelves free of all
the procrastination built up
and make my packages of potential
something worth considering again.

But as I continue to list
the job requirements,
I see that these are really
problems for the owner to fix.

Umbrellas

Rain never really goes away
it just constantly changes form
over and over,
without permission.
This taught me that
you have to be crazy
to think the sun will always shine

Aisle 6

Years from now,
if we ever run into
one another, I hope we
both can say that
who we moved on to
was best for us.

I'd hate to see
that either one of us
were looking for each other
in somebody else.

To Whoever This Was Written For

I'm waiting for the day
that I can tell you about
how you made me feel
the first time we met.

Maybe I'll be at the store
getting something I forgot to get
yesterday, or maybe I'll be
out with my friends that
finally dragged me out the house.

And then we'll see each other.
And I'll tell you about how
my heart had a fight with
my torso, won by a landslide
and proceeded to summersault
out of my chest and into
the palms of your hands.

I'll tell you how it felt like
God decided to pause everything
around me, and the smile
featured on your face
was the most perfect freeze frame
I've ever laid eyes on

I'll tell you about how the
only words I could think of
were forever, always, and eternity

but lumps in my windpipe
was my courage choking me
just at the mere thought
of you saying "hello."

I'll tell you about how I planned
the next 60 years of my life
with you in it in less
than 60 seconds and how
every woman that wasn't related
to me became completely irrelevant

I'll tell you about how I knew
that I loved you before I
knew I loved you and my
only focus was how fast
I could make you feel the same way

Then, I'll revisit how my first steps
towards you felt like steps you take
in a plane towards the door
right before you skydive

And when I finally spoke up
and you replied with the same
smile that made time stand still,
I've been falling through the sky ever since

Don't Judge

Your past is beyond my control
but our future isn't.
So by telling myself
I'm somehow capable
of looking at what you've done
with permission to judge,
I have to first ask myself
how well would my own past
stand trial

Accidents

You can't continue
to turn a blind eye
to red lights and stop signs
and always end up wondering
why you find yourself
in the middle of an accident

Eyez

She said her favorite part of me was my eyes,
when she first said it I was kinda surprised,
usually you get replies like smile or mind,
but not this time.
She told me it was my eyes.

I guess she noticed how they
never were able to lie

No matter how I said I felt or what
smile I ever tried to hide behind,
if she ever needed any answers
she just looked in my eyes.

She saw how they told my story,
from my dark stare of past failures,
to the way my eyes tend to spark
when I speak from my heart.
So I guess the saying that eyes
are the gateways to the soul has truth it still holds.

She knew that when I was quiet,
even my silence possessed energy
so in order for her to find my mind,
she first had to climb behind my eyes.

She knew that's where she'd find me,
behind all my bullshit and void of insecurities.
She'd find everything she needed to see,

from every word that I ever failed to speak,
to what was really on my mind
that I could never quite describe
when she'd ask what I was thinking about.

That's always been a hard question for me to answer.

But for some reason when I looked
at her she saw something I wasn't aware was there,
I never knew I was giving
my life away with every stare.

Or then again it could've been
only because she really cared,
and found a way to navigate
through every unyielding gaze,
 right to the doorstep of the place
 where my very essence laid.

She found a way to get to me through me,
and apparently I gave myself away

And she did it all just by looking in my eyes.

Lovers of Last Lifetime

I often wonder who loved me in my past life,

I wonder if we crossed paths right now would our scent
or our eyes or our voices being intertwined as we
unknowingly reintroduce ourselves,

 ring bells.

I wonder if every other person that came before you was
meant to be for reason or for seasons that they were never
able to live through, because they didn't do to me what
you did,

 when our love once lived

Maybe we remember how it all ended,

the day one of us left our love unfinished and created our
soul's search for revival with only one chance to fix our
mistakes,

or maybe we've already crossed paths and burnt bridges
and already it's too late

Maybe we died tragically together and our last words
were vows to come back and search Earth for each other's
eyes even if it took forever.

Maybe we were teens that didn't know anything other
than genuine love and life's circumstances shifted beyond
our control and separated us

And before we left we said we promise to never to love
another again,

Even if we have to live through sleepless nights and
countless wrongs until once again we're right where we
left off

But what if our paths never again cross?

What if one of us took bad directions along the way and
got lost?

What if our smiles never saw each other's eyes and our
fingers were never meant to be twice intertwined,

What if our hearts weren't supposed to stay confined to
the other's soul beyond our time that was already spent,

and what if we were only meant,

 to be lovers of last lifetime

11:42 PM

One of my biggest fears in life
is spending all this time
helping others meet the best
versions of themselves
while I'm only a shell of mine

I'm Not A Man

I'm not a man,
not in the physical sense
but in the sense of me
having your heart, and not
being man enough to know what to do with it.

I shoved it in my back pocket
with the rest of them,
and carried on with my life,
never taking a second
to look back at the trail of blood
left behind my steps

I continued with my boyish ways
seeing how many I could
collect and neglect, until one day
I looked behind me and
witnessed what resembled a murder scene

And that's the moment I realized
that I'm not a man yet.
A real man is not a hurter,
but a healer.

And all the time that I used others
in order to try to heal myself,
I never acknowledged the trail
I left behind myself
before I was a man

Unfinished

I've written hundreds of poems,
but all the ones I wrote about you
I never finish.
My hands clam up,
and the butterflies you leave in my stomach
turn into an angry nest of hornets
following every trace of your scent in my pen
stinging me with every letter of your name
every time I find courage to turn what
I feel about you into words.

My mind starts to race as if I'm trying
to outrun the thought of you,
but I always seem to stumble
on the image of your smile and you catch me
effortlessly.
My heart beats as if it's ready to jump out my chest
and into your hands and that way
the last place it can always say it was is with you.
I try to put my mind towards other things
that I could possibly write about,
other things that don't involve
this near death experience that comes
along with every time my voice
echoes your name when I close this notebook.

So if you ever come across
any poem I've written that's unfinished,
chances are it was about you.

90s R&B

If the love ain't like 90s R&B, keep it away from me

That Jodeci come and talk to me love, that let me call
you on the house phone and talk about nothing for
extremely long love,

The love that turns Boys to Men when I make love to
you in hopes that we never see the end of the road,

and if you do decide to go I'll be on bended knee until
you decide to come back to me.

That miseducation of Lauryn Hill love that painted it
like a perfect portrait,

that killing me softly ready or not because here I
come love, that love where you'll make a fool of
yourself and don't care who stares love

that SWV weak in the knees and ain't too proud to
beg like Keith Sweat for your TLC, that love that
made Dru Hill feel 5 steps away from eternity

That D'Angelo brown sugar shit, admiring every
sway of your hips and the fullness of your lips,

that 112 type of love where the only person
responsible for this could only be Cupid

That Mary J I'm going down real love but right before I hit the ground first like Maxwell I must admire this woman's work.

That love that makes you reminisce and this must be what Janet meant when she said that's the way love goes love,

that Tevin Campbell can we talk love where nothing else exists in that moment but us.

If when we look into each other's eyes and don't hear K-Ci and Jo Jo singing All My Life then it's not right, that's not the love for us.

If you don't hear our soul's melodies harmonizing in the background when we make love, that's not the love for us.

If I don't think of any of these things when I think of us, it may be time to find another love

And for another person I'll never be able to speak, but for me personally,

if it don't feel like 90s R&B, it ain't the love for me.

Black Love Is Wack

When did it become wack to love a black woman?

Why is it that we've been taught to think that it was
something wrong with upholding our own queens?

Now I know the tv and magazines glorify the best
examples of worst shit to admire in a black woman

And taught the men that the more the merrier and
"b****es ain't shit"

So both parties fell victim to a trick of the system, and
were made to believe that loving our woman was
unaspiring

Why is it that we act like if we all had daughters we
wouldn't wanna show her better,

instead of superficial admiration and misguided
persuasion into thinking the essence of a black woman is
anything short of magic and they naturally have it

Little black girls growing up under the impression that
it's a crime to possess melanin, and the only way to attract
is to alter the perfection they're born possessing

Little black boys growing to think that disrespect and
selling dreams that they always neglect is the recipe of an
acceptable man

But who are we to blame when they learned it watching
us, and to not be part of the solution equates to aid the

agenda of black woman hate

Our future fathers and mothers need to understand they
were made like no other and a healthy black family is the
most powerful tool of all humanity.

So love our black women,

cherish the most resilient, strongest, beautiful, boldest
human being that inherits this earth that was fooled into
compromising their own true beauty and worth

Loving a black woman ain't wack to me and will never be,

but somewhere along the line we were made to think it
was wack to think like that.

Insomnia

It's always when it's late,
right before my mind meets sleep
and is almost at ease,
you visit me right before my dreams.

Your scent is still on my pillow,
traces of your soul still wrapped in my covers,
cold sheets once warmed by the passion
that we shared with each other.

This bed was our fortress,
it's where we loved through fights,
and held each other through sleepless nights

This bed, is where our souls intertwined while our
bodies would reside.

If I'm quiet enough I can still hear your voice in my
window's wind,
soft whispers with words that erased inhibitions and
fears when you were here.

But now it always seems to trail off and disappear.

I toss and turn on what used to be your side hoping
to feel your energy next to me,
hoping to roll over to your hair in my face or your
hands reaching back to grab mine to bring me closer
to you

And now I see that maybe, I should've held on a little tighter.

As I lay in a nostalgic daze while memories in my mind continuously play,

I see the sky getting lighter and the sun beating you back home again.

And my journey through our imaginary remission brought me all the way back to my current position

An unrested mind and bloodshot eyes left love and sleep deprived.

But I begin my day like everything's just fine.

Take Me Back

Take me back to when I was too young to dread Mondays and when I thought beer was disgusting

Take me back to where I thought I had it all figured out, too naive to ever doubt myself and full of the audacity to believe that I could really be anything

Take me back to when I didn't know what a bill was and money didn't matter and my occupations consisted of playing outside and not letting the streetlights beat me home

Take me back to my first kiss, my first heartbreak, and the first time I thought true love was exchanged by hugs in between classes and hours on the house phone

Back to when I had all my friends in class that one year and even that other year when I ended up with that one teacher they told you to fear,

that little half square half triangle pizza and that other cafeteria shit we swear we hated,

but in the end we always ate it.

When church wasn't optional and my hobbies included walking through stores with mamma window shopping

"And I bet' not touch anything unless I had "anything" money"

When we only thought we were grown but little did we know that maybe we shouldn't have been in such a rush to grow old

We should've listened when they told us to live a little slower, not to take as many things granted, and things won't always go how we planned

Take me back to the childish sleep that contained all my tallest dreams,

take me back to a place where life's mistakes also gave me my greatest advice

Let me relive it all from every sin to every win, I promise I won't change it

Just let me do it again..

Iso

I'm learning to be alone,

and that's scary because
I've always been taught
that there's somebody
for everybody.

But what if my somebody
doesn't make it through everybody?

Or what if neither do I?

Fear

I fear that my time in this world may have meant to be spent differently.

I fear that my potential and what others see won't be to what I ever amount,

and my search for purpose will leave me with a life led seeking something never found.

I'm scared that my introverted ways pushed away one too many chances at love,

that I lost loyalty to pride because I was never able to take it out of my heart and put it aside at times.

I fear losing time with family on selfish endeavors of self-discovery will never be reclaimed,

and my inability to constantly express my undying endearment permanently hindered our relationships.

I'm scared that my past will outrun my future,

that my creativity will one day leave and these words will lose their ability to flow from me,

and before I die I won't get to leave my story behind for the eyes that need to see.

I fear that a fatherless home will affect my ability to ever be the one that I never got to learn from,

and a flawed past featuring endless falls will guide future failures.

I'm scared that what I've accomplished has reached its climax.

I fear that it won't end like I want,
and I'll be left with nothing but pieces in the end,

that all the bridges I crossed will be burned before we make amends.

I fear a life being lived inferior, and the weight that I carry with me will be too heavy.

I fear being too patient, but fear rushing the journey and missing moments that matter most

Fear that my perception won't reflect in my reflection,

Fear that the road I've traveled may not be headed in the right direction.

Fear that my eyes will close before my heart opens,

and that before it's all over my most important words will be left unspoken.

Alterations

We often make the mistake of thinking
that the way we love someone
is one size fits all,
instead of acknowledging that
in order to be a perfect fit for another
sometimes alterations have to be made

Reciprocity

Reciprocity is a two way street
that most only travel down one way.
We expect so much from others,
but of ourselves our requirements
are never as steep.

The Government is Watching Reality TV

Turn on your tv, and for yourself you can see exactly how it's going down.

They glorify everybody that glorifies what they need to keep us in captivity.

They tell us all day:

"All you can do is hoop and rap or if you're funny make me laugh with your comedy acts,

but that's about all we need to hear from you niggas.

So this is what I'm gonna do,

the only things I'm gonna allow you to see when you look around you are the following:

We'll make your rappers look like superheroes,

give them enough money to promote our message that it matters more about your money and clothes than what you actually know.

Let's make sure we throw a few athletes in there too to limit the potential of their views,

if you can't entertain us then sell drugs because that's the only thing else left for you.

As for their women, let's give them a few reality shows to show them they can't be worth anything without a fat ass

146

and weave that's 22 inches.

Make sure you show them doing nothing more than fighting over men and using every filter in a different club to cover insecurities every weekend

Make them wish their skin was lighter, their hair was straighter,

that if it doesn't involve their looks then it's not a good look because that's the only thing we tricked niggas into acknowledging anyway.

Don't let them see their own kind positively attached to anything ,

don't let them see that they're capable to think with any depth or complexity.

Don't let them see that they are able to succeed if they made a conscious effort to redirect their energy and build up their communities.

And when you do all of this make sure you do it quietly, don't let them know that they're still sleep.

So let's use this recipe on every channel, every phone screen, and inside every magazine.

And If we do all these things correctly,

at the bottom is where they will always stay."

Shine

Everybody has a light,

We all shine differently and yours may appear to not always be as bright,

but there's always light.

We've all been guilty of dimming ourselves for others at times, or even allowing our own minds to be the reason we refuse to shine,

We've all lied, we've all cried, we've all had moments where pride pushed our light aside in order to let forced feelings reside in the way of loving our lives,

but through every crack created from unpleasant times, your light still shines

We were never meant to pursue perfection because all along we've always possessed it,

We never needed direction, but instead to trust the path we already have.

We never had to search for light because we already were given it behind our very own eyes,

we never need to figure out who we would be, but instead who we already are, and we're all stars.

No matter the moments that make minds misguide
us from realizing how special we can be,

living in the shadows and not chasing your passion is
never the life we were meant to lead.

And some find comfort in shade as long as they can
sit in peace,

but we were all meant step from under our trees and
live out who we were meant to be for the world to
see.

Don't ever let them tell you that you're inferior, never
let them tell you that you weren't meant to be great.

Never let another that doesn't have to live your life be
the decider of your fate.

The longer we wait for breaks, dimming your light
could be the reason another that needs to see you
shine, loses their way

So if nobody told you today, know that you're worth
it and there's no need to feel like your light was never
meant to shine.

Stop wasting time.

Naked

I wanna see you naked,
but don't touch what you're wearing.
First take off your apprehension
and leave it laying at the door.
Take your insecurities and every fear
of feeling inferior and let them
fall to the floor.
Unbutton your past and pull down
your pessimistic views that all
these other men
before me, left you in.
Let me see what you look like
when you don't have anything on
that keeps me from what I wanna see
The only thing I wanna see you in
is your own skin
so I can look at every blemish
or imperfection you think
that you possess, look you in the
center of your soul, and tell you
that naked and all,
you're still just as beautiful.

Full Circle

Karma comes full circle,
and it's never up to us
to decide if the circle is
narrow or wide,
but never forget
that eventually it'll find
its way back around

Last Conversation

I wish that our last conversation
wasn't our last conversation.
In a moment we tore down
what took us forever to build
choosing not to figure it out
but instead to be finished.
Wiping our hands clean of one another
but stains on our fingers remain.
We took back the pieces we put in place
and exposed the same voids we once filled
and reopened scars that we once
were the reason why they healed.

Standing Rain

Many can't stand the rain
but personally, I've always
loved the idea of the
fresh start that comes
along with it

An Empath's Journey

The longer I'm alive,
I realize
I was put here for you,
even more than for me.
And my empathy has turned out to be
my best and worst quality.
I feel everybody and everything.
To the point where I think,
a vessel is what I was meant to be.

I always found beauty
in the most unlikely of people and places,
and spent a lot of time taking in the pain
from all different hearts and faces.
Tears have flown from my eyes
that were never my own to own,
but instead,
for the burden of another that I chose to bear.

I wasn't put here for me.
But instead to ease your journey,
to claim some of the baggage you can't,
to help heal the pain that you daily conceal.

Even if it means I conceal my own forever,
because putting myself second in a world so selfish,
has left me with next to nothing,
except more empathy.

Custom Fit

We get everything custom fit for our failure,
and they ask us why we can't succeed.

They can't even see the things we're forced to defeat
before we try to succeed outside of our own
communities.

They put us in projects to see their project, stacking
black families in 1 bedroom closets,

and they deposit the drugs and guns like they were
made by us, but I've never seen a nigga make a rifle or
harvest those seeds those drugs are made of.

Our schools are filled with secondhand shit from 1966
that they've cared less to update since Brown vs. Board
of Education

and those tattered books they put in our face every day
to memorize every page, are written by crooks that
stole history, and turned black truth into black misery

and filled it with false white achievements while
whiting out their sins that can't be related to by
anybody in a classroom full of young black kids

as they get lectured to by somebody that looks
nothing like them.

They take away the funding for facilities in the same communities where those same kids live,

and leave nothing but a park with a basketball hoop so that from an early age all they know how to do is run fast, jump high, and shoot with every pun intended

They only use us for concerts and game(s), with their most recent being how many of them they can kill that look ridiculously similar to me on camera to win a two week vacation before being found not guilty.

They literally give every other race property in our space and take every other one of us away and make them property of the state,

And every leader we seem to get, the ones that used their voice to actually make a difference and awaken lost souls around them,

if you write them all down and take your pick out of a hat, find me one that didn't die of a bullet

They give us all of this, custom fit, and ask us why it's so hard to do anything with it.

Already Was

Everything I need to succeed is already given to me,

lying dormant on my soul's doormat patiently
waiting on me to claim my package.

But for a while, everything was backwards.

I was looking for things I never possessed in hopes of
one day poking my chest out once my conquest came
to an end.

But after a while I grew tired, not understanding that
this journey was designed to never see an end,
because the destination that I had been chasing my
whole life,

was within.

The objective was never to figure out what or who I
would or could be, but instead who I already was.

Quiet

My natural silence has been a gift
as well a curse.
Being my savior in some instances
and in others my downfall.
The words that I never said,
just as loud as the ones you heard.

Used to Love Me

The problem was,
you used to love me
before I loved myself.
So even when I thought
I loved you, I lost you
because I never knew
loving another was impossible
until I learned how to love me first.

Wish List

It's funny how the things we wished for
when we were younger
were things that money could buy.
Now everything on my wish list
are a bunch things that not even
a person of infinite riches
would ever have the luxury
of being able to afford.

Water

If I could be like anything,
I'd be like water.
Flexible enough to survive
every twist and turn
with relative ease
without ever breaking,
even when I'm stretched
to my thinnest.

Formless enough,
to no longer fit in boxes
custom made and labeled
as my destiny's container
and able to take shape
of the solution to any problem

Strong enough,
to wipe out cities of fear
and demolish the little
beach houses of doubt
that my mind at times
builds along its own coastline.

But all the while,
choosing peace
as my natural preferred state

A Dream for Black Men Only

Last night I had a dream,
I was at the park one evening
sitting in a field watching the clouds,
and out of nowhere, an endless
amount of police officers appeared.
For some reason they all had guns
drawn and pointed towards me
and their SWAT gear looked
as if they were called to alleviate
a riot or had a dangerous home to raid.
But instead, all of their aggression
was being thrown in my direction.
I put my hands up the same time
that my heart dropped to my shoelaces,
not because I had done anything wrong
but because I knew my skin alone
came inherited with a felony
that carried the death sentence
everywhere I went, and another
chargeable offense wasn't needed
for my life to end right then.
All I saw around me were scowling
white faces and every time I blinked
their masks turned into white hooded sheets
as they screamed at me,
I'll never forget those screams.
They told me to start crawling
towards them and I better not look up
and I did exactly what they said

in fear that if I didn't,
that was enough permission
for my life to be ended.
As I got closer, they told me
to stand up slowly, and as I
stood up to face my fate,
I heard deafening sounds
of loaded clips of ammunition
and saw nothing but the light
of a thousand guns
with their bullets set on me.

And at that exact moment,
I woke up with tear filled eyes
thinking that I had witnessed
my own innocent demise
that would prematurely end my life.
And as I exhaled a relief filled sigh,
I realized,

this was only a dream that a black man could have.

Love Hurt

Why is it, that most of us
have a terrible habit
of loving people that hurt us
only to turn around
and hurt people that love us.

11/02/1990

If you leave me,
don't expect to come back
and see that everything
is exactly the same

If you leave me,
I promise you change
will be taking your place

Only a fool won't turn
a loss into a lesson
so whenever a loss was evident
I found a way to make
progress out of pain
and turn a loss into change

So you can leave if you'd like
but please understand
that if you try to come back
don't be surprised
if you can't find me

Don't Wait

Don't wait for me to get my life together
before I decide to love you better.
Don't wait on my potential to arrive
at your doorstep and deliver the version of me
you deserved gift wrapped with your name
in fancy gold letters on the tag

Don't wait for my actions and words
to become identical twins when usually
at best they resemble distant relatives
causing a war between your eyes and your ears

Don't wait for me to figure it out
while our love floats on clouds of doubt
due to my inability to be the man
you need me to be.

I'd much rather see you be free.

10:29 PM

My relationships lately have been
like beautiful flowers
with short lifespans.

No matter what I've done
to try and keep them alive
the only thing that seems to decide
when it dies, is the season.

Still Nigga

I turn on the news and see nothing but the blues, but every now and then this is something that they'll do,

put a few niggas of contrasting views on a segment and let them argue about what they think niggas should do.

They make sure one was Ivy League schooled and followed all the rules, living his life Europeanized and always doing what he was "supposed to do."

Watching the things he'll say to make sure that the sleeping never wake,

rocking them away with accepted Uncle Tom ways, when they wouldn't even be at your funeral if he died today.

One that thought civil rights and equality already came, and our people still don't suffer from the effects of slavery today

The type to be hanging at the country club and say, something wild like "I'm not black, I'm OJ"

A man who has no clue that a degree can't validate you, and they accept him not out of want but because they have to

But at the end of the day, you're still just another nigga too.

And the other is usually completely different,

a rapper or another prominent figure whose message is usually something that's glorified but not meant to fall on the ears of our children.

It probably promotes drugs, staying lit, and keeping hoes, but how can you promote what you're not shown if this is all a nigga knows

He was probably on the Gram holding money to his ear, but we ain't take the time to wonder how the disconnect appeared.

He probably brought a few V-12 engines anyway, because he was never taught to invest in things that appreciate

Probably came from the hood like from where a few of us came, but we don't realize that's the place most our people STILL are today.

And that place breeds a mentality that's seldom overcame, after seeing your parents do drugs and your best friends slain or chained.

No role models there because it's hard to get saved, when your teacher tells you that you're a failure in 7th grade.

So he raps his way out the hood by telling his point of view, telling the harsh truths of his youth for the masses to view

Yet his influence is the biggest on what most of us do.

And by the time they're done with the interviews, the ones watching for guidance and clues are left even more lost and confused.

With no advice on what to do because all two men could do, was waste time belittling the other's point of view

All while a white man sits & moderates, like he could ever narrate a story that perpetuates anything else other than subliminal black hate.

A man that's never seen the projects, let alone been there, so why would he give a damn what happens, why would he care?

The type that probably endorsed another candidate, but on Election Day "accidentally" pressed Trump anyway

And he claims that he can "emphasize" with your pain, but really if it doesn't fall into the white agenda he stays away

So when the time is up and there's nothing left to say, his ratings went up and his show got the fame,

even though all he saw was just two niggas arguing anyway.

Today

One day, you wake up
and realize that time
won't always be on your side.
You notice that tomorrow
won't always be yours to have
and yesterdays can't keep
ending the same way
as you let your time
walk out the door
with no intentions
of ever being yours again.

A change can't be made
being consumed by past mistakes
or future daydreams,
but only in the choice you make today.

So let today be the day
you decide to change.
Love today, live today,
face fears today, laugh more today,
challenge yourself and chase your passion,
give the world you in its best form today,
and be the reason good energy reciprocates.
Find peace today, and if possible
help someone else do the same.

But please never forget,
that the only time in your life
that you can ever change,
is today.

1:58 PM

My emotions
are like a brick wall some days,
and others like quicksand.

8 To 28

When I was a kid,
the world didn't start living
in the palms of their hands yet
and even though communication
wasn't as constant,
people felt a little closer.

Texting was taking time
to write a letter
Facebook used to be phone calls
and Instagram took the place
of conversations face to face

Our neighbors weren't strangers,
and even if we don't have
our memories stored online
they seem to be just as vivid.

Limerence

Getting married for anything
other than love
is like building a sandcastle
on the shore, hoping
that it stays intact

Why I Deleted My Tinder

The fact that we live in a generation
that has the audacity to feel
entitled to so much,
we can right and left swipe
casually through each other's lives

And the fact that I was
on Tinder when these words
ran through my mind
lets me know I'm part of it too.

Teach The Kids

We need to teach our black boys
you make more money
by being smart than you do
being strong and fast

and our black girls
that magic resides inside
that black skin
and that the world imitates them,
not the other way around

Tears For Trayvon

I cried for Trayvon tonight.
I cried because he looked
so much like my little brother.
And no matter if
I taught him everything that
I knew was right,
I could never teach him
how to not be a target
when his God given complexion
is a bullseye he'll never have the luxury
of removing from his chest.

I could never teach him
that even when he does
nothing wrong, there's a
chance that hate will choose
to show up on his doorstep
with no intentions of a friendly visit

I could never teach him
that no amount of money
no amount of success
no amount of education or white friends
will ever be able to change how
they really view you in a place
you were never meant to survive.

And I cried.
I cried because as strong

as I considered myself to be,
as much as I know I can bear
I still felt helpless and weak

because as a black man
you can do everything right
and still lose your life.

Freedom Fighters

17.3% of the military
is African American.
I always found this odd
because 0% of them
are fighting for a country
that they are free in.

Spring Cleaning

I'm a mess.

A collection of right turns that should've been lefts combined with a few stumbles over necessary steps that I didn't take

I know my family's proud of me and the people I love see success and seem to look beyond this unmade bed which is my life,

   but all I see, is this mess.

Everybody says that at this point in my life it's cool not have it all figured out and patience is a virtue

   but those same ones will tell you tomorrow's not promised in the same breath, so as for today...

This mess is all I see.

Things all over the floor for every test of life I took and failed with flying colors,

   stained mirrors and dirty showers filled with the epitome of what I see of me in this present time,

   a person that can't see himself clearly stumbling through unfulfilled purpose collecting dirt of hopelessness that I wash off daily

And it seems the more I try to clean up, I look around and

find something else that's out of place.

Dirty dishes representing past mistakes that I have been too scared to go near

A basket overflowing with clothes that should've been washed days ago shows the procrastination that I add to life daily.

So I start cleaning...

scrubbing every wall, counter, and window until I can begin to see my inner peace again under all my insecurity

But no matter what vacuum called this fake smile I use daily to suck people into believing that I think this room in my mind is nice and neat,

no matter what broom called these good intentions I use to sweep every corner hoping that eventually I'll see the results

No matter what mop called this heart of mine that I use to soak up every spill and stain hoping that I'll never have to do this again,

I know it'll only be a matter of time before I'll be spring cleaning again.

Real Relationship's Rubric

I need you to be the reason for a few things in my life that others have tried to be and ended up thinking differently..

I need you to be the reason I believe in my own definition of love, because the older I get my idea now seems identical with a nice part of some shit from movie scripts

I need you to make me believe in glass slippers again

I need you to be my reciprocity,

　　seeing what I see even when at times when fog might appear to cloud the vision around my dreams, I need you to be my high beams.

I need you to be my life's diary,

For your eyes only, be the scroll that holds all my secrets, all my weird tendencies and all the reasons I look at things a little differently,

　　but you never hold them against me because you know that though I'm slow to expose myself, thoughts that flow from my soul have always been my greatest form of wealth.

I need you to be able to read my eyes, and not rely on words at all times because a man will at times say less when feeling more, and I need you to understand.

I need you to be the reason phone locks no longer exist and when we do choose to coexist I need you to be my copilot on life's trip because I've had enough passengers

I need you to be the reason I know heaven exists, because only a gift so perfect, so worth it, so handcrafted for me could only be made purposefully from nothing but prayers and dreams

I need you to be the exception to every double standard, be my eraser that helps me make corrections and be my mirror when I'm wrong to show me the errors in my reflection

I need your patience, I need your passion, your words followed by identical actions with no retractions from our love's faction...

I need you to be my soul's vacation and my heart's oasis.

I understand if what I need you to be can be seen as a task unforeseen by many women, but it should be because regardless of who may read, these words are only intended for one

And I'm not sure if this is anything she will ever even lay eyes on and see, but I need you to be these things...

And the main reason is because these are all the things that for you, I also plan to be...

Conversations With God

I talk to God a lot,

even though I never knew who he was, or even if he is she and everything we were told to believe isn't even what it may be

and I'm not saying it's all a lie, I'm saying I don't know..

I don't think God cares about Catholic, Mormon, Baptist, Buddhist, Presbyterian, or Pentecostal labels used as human segregation with similar stories and moral filled fables to judge another based on faith,

But I hope God cares more about the man regardless of belief,

with a good heart and genuine love given being the main keys to please our creator even if we made a few miscues along the way

I think God gets mistakes.

I don't think God wrote a Bible or a Quran, or if a book was even written..

But I do know a Bible was carried on ships by Europeans and used as a tool to rule and manipulate many African kingdoms into blind submission

I pray a lot,

even though I don't know exactly who I'm praying to or if my prayers are even heard,

But I pray anyway.

I pray for everybody, from the people I love most to strangers I simply walk past,

because I don't think God ever cared about race, religion, or how much time you spent in church filling offering plates

And I don't know what awaits after our life here sees its expiration date.

But I hope God cares more for the time of gratitude spent & amount of good energy reciprocated as more important things to ensure a fortunate fate

I don't know what it is or who we'll answer to or if the person we've been answering to is our own conscience all along

I don't know exactly what it is that keeps my heart grateful and my sanity stable regardless of life's challenges

I talk to God a lot, and though our conversation always tends to leave him speechless,

I'm thankful, for whoever it is that hears my heart speaking.

Lovers of Last Lifetime

I often wonder who loved me in my past life,

I wonder if we crossed paths right now would our scent or our eyes or our voices being intertwined as we unknowingly reintroduce ourselves,

ring bells.

I wonder if every other person that came before you was meant to be for reason or for seasons that they were never able to live through, because they didn't do to me what you did,

when our love once lived

Maybe we remember how it all ended,

the day one of us left our love unfinished and created our soul's search for revival with only one chance to fix our mistakes,

or maybe we've already crossed paths with burnt bridges and already it's too late

Maybe we died tragically together and our last words were vows to come back and search Earth for each other's eyes even if it took forever.

Maybe we were teens that didn't know anything other than genuine love and life's circumstances shifted beyond our control and separated us

And before we left we said we promise to never love another again,

Even if we have to live through sleepless nights and countless wrongs until once again we're right...

where we left off

But what if our paths never again cross?

What if one of us took bad directions along the way and got lost?

What if our smiles never saw each other's eyes and our fingers were never meant to be twice intertwined,

What if our hearts weren't supposed to stay confined to the other's soul beyond our time that was already spent,

and what if we were only meant,

to be lovers of last lifetime

Dashon's Interlude

I know if it was up to you, I would still be that little boy holding your hand as we crossed streets.

If it was up to you, my car seat would still be in your rearview and I'd be talking your head off asking you those annoying kid questions like

"Mommy why is the sky blue, mommy where do babies come from, mommy why do you always make me go to bed so early on Christmas Eve"

until you get tired and tell me to be quiet, either that or I always eventually fell asleep.

I think you'd even take me back at that weird adolescent phase, where I thought I was so ready to tackle life and had not the slightest idea of why me being so eager to be independent was your biggest fear.

I remember the day I went to college, you were the last person I saw and as you embraced me with tear swelled eyes and we both cried together for the first time in our lives. That was the first time I ever saw you cry, and that was the first time I understood.

I was no longer that little boy holding your hand, asking questions, and depending on you as if the essence of life itself was held in your hands....I was a man

But if it was up to me, part of me will always wish I was still that little boy too.

Writer's Block

I have a notebook full of unfinished poems...

Full of words that a lot of times feel like small pieces of my soul leaving the depths of my heart never to be mine again...

so when I do actually finish a poem I've always considered it an accomplishment,

it usually takes a lot

Poems about the people I know, the places I've seen, and the things that I've been through...

My life is transitioning,

for the longest I felt like I was living to write and now I'm slowly starting to feel like I'm writing to live

Quickly learning that it's impossible for one man to keep so much of himself inside of himself and not expect to suffocate

For most of my life the thought of sharing my countless flaws with anyone other than myself was always considered a bad idea,

and aside from you and me there's a reason not too many people do so willingly

Why would I want the world to know that no matter

what people think about me I'm still insecure, still unsure about what they see that I don't?

Why would I want the world to know that the more I try to be with another I always would feel like they deserve someone better no matter how much they tell me they think otherwise?

Why would I ever want the world to know that my life is anything other than perfect on purpose?

And then I doubt my words...

So right before I get to the point where I build up the courage to finish that final stanza and say the line that's most necessary

I always find a reason to stop...

telling myself that nobody will ever be able to understand my story no matter how I choose to tell it

So I just stop writing

Made in the USA
Columbia, SC
04 November 2022

70432535R00109